Music Minus One Trumpet
or Flugelhorn

Mostly Mozart

Opera Arias with Orchestra

6850

- notes continued from back cover

If you've purchased any of my MMOs with songs from the Great American Song Book, you know that I'm an advocate of learning the lyrics and hence the stories of the songs in order to express the music with emotion.

However, working with these great arias, I had to settle for just a basic understanding of the roles, dramatically speaking. Of course, if you're curious you are invited to research the operatic settings for these arias.

With that said, my approach with Papageno's whimsical aria was simply to enter a bit more intensity to each subsequent verse.

With ***O Isis und Osiris*** also from The Magic Flute I chose the Flugelhorn for the "voice" of this lovely chorale-like aria where Papageno sings about a mythological character. Notice that this melody appears simple but as in all of Mozart's compositions it is deceptive for he had a very subtle way of introducing complexity without being obvious!

Voi, che sapete che cosa e amor ("You, who know what love is") from the Marriage Of Figaro has such an exquisite quality to explore. I urge you to immerse yourself in its extraordinary melodic and harmonic beauty. Enough said!

Tardi s'avvede d'un Tradimento ("Later she understands of treason") from La Clemenza di Tito like O Isis und Osiris suggested the French horn to me so I chose the Flugelhorn for this aria in 3/4 time which has almost the lilt of a minuet.

The next aria presents an interesting contrast between vocal and instrumental music. Well, at least from my perspective in trying to "translate" or adapt opera or musical drama into the rather abstract world of instrumental music.

Smanie Implacabili means Torments Implacable which is sung by Dorabella a mezzo-soprano in Cosa Fan Tutte. In this scene Dorabella is bemoaning her torment at being left alone by her betrothed and her maid Despina advised her to take new lovers while her betrothed is away!

Now, as much as I'd like to be able to express the emotions of this scene, far be it from me to presume that I can communicate it with the trumpet!

This is how I viewed it: Mozart's compositions are so sublime and exquisitely crafted that even without the lyrics and dramatic content they are amazing works of Art and as such, I decided to let the Muses guide me in this instrumental version for trumpet and orchestra. To my surprise, I found this aria removed from its dramatic setting to have a heroic quality perfectly suited for the trumpet and voila! a transformation occurred!

I can only hope that my humble offering pleases the Great Master in Composer's Heaven.

Presto or Prestissimo should be the concept with ***Fin ch'han dal vino*** or ***The Champagne Aria*** ("Till they are tipsy") from Don Giovanni. If you think this is a fast tempo, go to YouTube and view Bryn Terfel sing it at the Metropolitan Opera. That's really fast and with tongue-twisting words to boot!

Now, here's an opportunity to slow down, be a Don Juan and serenade your love with ***Deh! vieni alla finestra*** (("Ah! come to the window".) Don Giovanni does this to an accompaniment of a mandolin which Mozart orchestrates so that it has an almost lute-like elegance.

I fell in love with ***No, la morte, io non pavento*** ("No, I'm not afraid of dying") from Idomeneo and there's nothing more to say than just let Mozart's absolute perfection guide you through this wonderful piece.

If you're up to the challenge you could play this on Bb or A piccolo trumpet or better still D trumpet for it's in D Major concert. I recorded an alternate version on Piccolo Trumpet in A which put me in the "friendliest" key of F Major but preferred this version on Bb Trumpet.

If you would like to explore playing these on Piccolo in A or D Trumpet, I'd be happy to email you the music. Of course, you could do it yourself and that would be good training in itself.

At this point, I introduced two pieces that are not Mozart's namely Rossini's elegant and pristine aria ***Sciocco...qual piacer*** ("Silly, what pleasure") from L'Italiana In Algeri and Schubert's masterpiece ***Ave Maria.***

This Rossini aria is an ideal trumpet or cornet solo and while rather technical compared to the others it almost rolls off the tongue in once again the key of Eb concert.

(Okay, I agree it will take more than a quick scan to get it to that point but keep in mind that before I transposed it from E Major, can you imagine how difficult it would have been in 6 sharps?)

What can I say about ***Ave Maria,*** a staple for vocal and instrumental soloists especially for church services and wedding ceremonies? Franz Schubert was a brilliant creator of song and an outstanding example is his Ave Maria. Here, you can enjoy the orchestral accompaniment and let it envelop you as you sing through the horn.

This last piece, although I like to think of it as my tribute to the Master of Salzburg is a departure from the rest of the album since it's a duet that I arranged. The source is an incredible collection called *Vocalises and Exercises for Soprano.* For years I've owned and played these unusual pieces that Mozart wrote for his young wife Constance (Weber) to serve as singing lessons! I've now taken the liberty of arranging a second part to create a duet for two trumpets. This is an excerpt from Vocalise #1 but in only a couple of minutes of music Mozart takes us through a kaleidoscopic tonal journey!

It is is a precursor to a forthcoming Music Minus One of Mostly Mozart Duets For Two Trumpets patterned after my Two-part Inventions and other Masterworks by Bach for Two Trumpets (MMO 6847).

For Vocalise #1 I'll use the same format of five versions of each duet:

A two trumpet version with a click count-off to listen to and individual parts to play along with that have a click track throughout for practice purposes and lastly the same with only a count-off and no click track to be used for performances.

Forgive my extreme adoration of Mozart's creations but he was undoubtedly a musical phenomenon! This Vocalise is an interesting example of a way to "practice" in the most aesthetically satisfying way!

A very wise man noted that Music came before exercises!

Along the same line of thinking, Adolph Herseth, the legendary principal trumpeter in the Chicago Symphony once said simply: "Never practice, always perform!" That axiom is on a card posted in my studio.

I am offering a complimentary Skype or FaceTime session to purchasers of this or any of my MMOs to help them get the maximum benefit.

I hope you get as much enjoyment from this album as I did creating it!

Robert Zottola
bobzottolamusic@comcast.net
Naples, Florida

Mostly Mozart

Opera Arias with Orchestra

CONTENTS

Complete Track	Minus Track			Page
	12	Bb Tuning Notes	(0:33)	
1	13	Der Vogelfänger bin ich ja *from The Magic Flute*	(2:43)	6
2	14	O Isis und Osiris *from The Magic Flute*	(2:53)	7
3	15	Voi, che sapete che cosa e amor *from The Marriage Of Figaro*	(2:52)	8
4	16	Tardi s'avvede d'un Tradimento *from La Clemenza di Tito*	(2:34)	9
5	17	Smanie Implacabili *from Cosi fan Tutte*	(1:48)	10
6	18	Fin ch'han dal vino *from Don Giovanni*	(1:45)	12
7	19	Deh vieni alla finestra *from Don Giovanni*	(1:48)	14
8	20	No, la morte io non pavento *from Idomeneo*	(1:51)	16
9	21	Sciocco… qual piacer *from L'Italiana in Algeri*	(3:21)	18
10	22	Ave Maria *from Ellen Gesang III (Ellen's Third Song)*	(5:06)	21
11	23	Vocalise No. 1 (Trumpet 1 with Click) *from Vocalises and Exercises for Soprano*	(1:54)	22
	24	Vocalise No. 1 (Trumpet 2 with Click)	(1:54)	22
	25	Vocalise No. 1 (Trumpet 1 without Click)	(1:54)	22
	26	Vocalise No. 1 (Trumpet 2 without Click)	(1:54)	22

ISBN 978-1-941566-86-2

Solo Bb Trumpet or Cornet

Der Vogelfänger bin ich ja

from *The Magic Flute*

W.A. Mozart
Edited by Robert Zottola

Andante

Solo Flugelhorn

O Isis und Osiris

from *The Magic Flute*

W.A. Mozart

Edited by Robert Zottola

Solo Bb Trumpet or Cornet

Voi, che sapete che cosa e amor

from *The Marriage of Figaro*

W.A. Mozart

Edited by Robert Zottola

Solo Flugelhorn

Tardi s'avvede d'un Tradimento

from *La Clemenza di Tito*

W.A.Mozart

Edited by Robert Zottola

Solo Bb Trumpet or Cornet

Smanie Implacabili

from *Cosi fan Tutte*

W.A. Mozart

Edited by Robert Zottola

Solo Bb Trumpet or Cornet

Fin ch'han dal vino

from *Don Giovanni*

W.A.Mozart
Edited by Robert Zottola

Fin ch'han dal vino

Solo Bb Trumpet or Flugelhorn

Deh vieni alla finestra

from *Don Giovanni*

W.A.Mozart

Edited by Robert Zottola

Other Trumpet Albums That Bob Zottola Has Created for Music Minus One

Brazilian Bossa Novas by Jobim ....MMO 3871
Bob Zottola, trumpet: The Girl From Ipanema • So Danco Samba • Once I Loved • Dindi • One Note Samba • Meditation • How Insensative • Triste • Corcovado • Wave

Standards for Trumpet, vol. 1 ....MMO 6841
Bob Zottola, trumpet: When You're Smiling • I'm In The Mood for Love • Blue Bossa • How Do You Keep The Music Playing? • It's Only A Paper Moon • Samba de Orfeo • Blue Moon • You Must Believe In Spring • Black Orpheus • Fly Me To The Moon

Standards for Trumpet, vol. 2 - "Pure Imagination" ....MMO 6842
Bob Zottola, trumpet: September In The Rain • Pure Imagination • I May Be Wrong • Here's That Rainy Day • This Happy Madness • Body and Soul • Smoke Gets In Your Eyes • Always • Embraceable You • I Got Rhythm

Standards for Trumpet, vol. 3 - "Gold Standards" ....MMO 6843
Bob Zottola, trumpet: If I Should Lose You • Darn That Dream • Too Marvelous For Words • I Concentrate On You • Teach Me Tonight • Gentle Rain • Three Little Words • That's All • Little White Lies • Have Yourself A Merry Little Christmas

Standards for Trumpet, vol. 4 - "Stardust" ....MMO 6844
Bob Zottola, trumpet: The Best is Yet To Come • I Had The Craziest Dream • Baubles, Bangles and Beads • Cinema Paradiso • Can't Take My Eyes Off Of You • My Funny Valentine • Brazil • Stardust • Oh, Lady Be Good • The Christmas Song

Standards for Trumpet, vol. 5 - "Arrangements by Riddle" ....MMO 6845
Bob Zottola, trumpet: You Make Me Feel So Young • Fools Rush In • My Baby Just Cares For Me • The More I See You • Everywhere You Go • When Your Lover Has Gone • Day In, Day Out • It's A Sin To Tell A Lie • Near You • You're Driving Me Crazy

Standards for Trumpet, vol. 6 - "The Fine Art of Ballad Playing" ....MMO 6846
Bob Zottola, trumpet: In The Wee Small Hours of The Morning • I'll Be Around • Dancing On The Ceiling • I'll Never Be The Same • It Never Entered My Mind • Can't We Be Friends • I See Your Face Before Me • I Get Along Without You Very Well • This Love Of Mine • What Is This Thing Called Love?

J.S.Bach: Two Part Inventions *(2 CD Set)* ....MMO 6847
Bob Zottola, trumpet: Two-Part Invention #4 in D minor • Minuet in F Major • Minuet #3 in D minor • Little Prelude in C Major • Gavotte in G minor • Minuet in A minor • Minuet in D minor • Gavotte in Eb Major • Minuet in E Major • Minuet in C minor • Two-Part Invention #1 in C Major (Slow version) • Two-Part Invention #1 in C Major (Fast version)

Let The Trumpet Sound For Christmas ....MMO 6848
Bob Zottola, trumpet: Have Yourself A Very Merry Christmas • Santa Claus Is Coming to Town • Silent Night • White Christmas • I'll Be Home For Christmas • Count Your Blessings • I've Got My Love To Keep Me Warm • The Christmas Song • The Christmas Waltz • What Are You Doing New Year's Eve

ARBAN'S Opera Arias for Trumpet & Orchestra ....MMO 6849
Bob Zottola, trumpet with Orchestra: La Donna è Mobile • Una Furtiva Lagrima • Di Tanti Palpiti • Merce, Dilette Amici • Quanto è Bella • Sempre Libera • Voilà Donc Le Triste • Oh! Come da Quel di Tutto • Vien Leonora • Mentre Contemplo Quel Volto Amato • O Quante Lacrime Timor • Dell'iniqua, Del Protervo • Or Tutti Sorgete Ministri Infernali • Raggio d'Amor Parea • Come, Innocente Giovane • Meco Tu Vieni • Di Tale Amor che Dirsi • Quando le Sere al Placido • Libiamo Ne'lieti Calici

Mostly Mozart: Opera Arias with Orchestra ....MMO 6850
Bob Zottola, trumpet: Der Vogelfänger bin ich ja • O Isis und Osiris • Voi, che sapete che cosa e amor • Tardi s'avvede d'un Tradimento • Smanie Implacabili • Fin ch'han dal vino • Deh vieni alla finestra • No, la morte io non pavento • Sciocco... qual piacer • Ave Maria • Vocalise No. 1

Nashville Classics for Trumpet ....MMO 6851
Bob Zottola, trumpet: You Don't Know Me • 9 to 5 • Green, Green Grass of Home • Lady • Night Life • Pretty Woman • Crazy • Last Date • Always On My Mind

Signature Series, vol. 1 - *famous vocal hits transcribed for trumpet* ....MMO 6853
Bob Zottola, trumpet: For All We Know • I Left My Heart In San Francisco • The Way We Were • Mack The Knife • Moon River • Georgia On My Mind • All The Way • What A Wonderful World

Signature Series, vol. 2 - *more famous vocal hits transcribed for trumpet* ....MMO 6854
Bob Zottola, trumpet: The Very Thought Of You • That Old Black Magic • Tenderly • Misty • Hey There • Prisoner Of Love • Love Dance • Here's To Life

Signature Series, vol. 3 ....MMO 6855
Bob Zottola, trumpet: Lullaby Of Birdland • When I Fall In Love • Why Don't You Do Right? • Ev'ry Time We Say Goodbye • You Don't Know Me • Steppin' Out With My Baby • Days Of Wine and Roses • God Bless The Child

Solo Bb Trumpet or Cornet

No, la morte io non pavento

from *Idomeneo*

W.A. Mozart
Edited by Robert Zottola

No, la morte

Solo Bb Trumpet or Cornet

Sciocco... qual piacer

from *L'Italiana in Algeri*

Gioacchino Rossini
Edited by Robert Zottola

Sciocco
57
61
65
68
71
74
Vivace
78
82
85
89
6
rit.

Solo Bb Trumpet or Cornet

Ave Maria

from Ellens Gesang III

Franz Schubert
Edited by Robert Zottola

Vocalise No. 1

from *Vocalises and Exercises for Soprano*

W.A.Mozart

Arranged for Two Trumpets by Robert Zottola

Vocalise No. 1

Vocalise No. 1

Transcription by Kevin Mauldin

Music Minus One
50 Executive Boulevard • Elmsford, New York 10523-1325
914-592-1188 • e-mail: info@musicminusone.com
www.musicminusone.com

MMO 6850

ISBN 978-1-941566-86-2